4.50

INTERCESSIONS AT WORSHIP

A Guide For Those Who Lead Them

INTERCESSIONS AT WORSHIP

A guide for those who lead them

COLIN SEMPER

MOWBRAY

Mowbray
A Cassell imprint
Villiers House, 41/47 Strand, London WC2N 5JE, England
387 Park Avenue South, New York, NY 10016–8810, USA

Intercessions for Use with the Order of Holy Communion Rite A
first published 1982
This enlarged edition first published 1992

British Library Cataloguing-in-Publication Data
A catalogue record for this book is available from the British
Library.

Library of Congress Cataloging-in-Publication Data
Available from the Library of Congress.

ISBN 0-264-67226-7

Typeset by Colset Private Ltd, Singapore
Printed and bound in Great Britain by
Biddles Ltd, Guildford and King's Lynn

CONTENTS

THE MEANING AND PURPOSE OF INTERCESSION

It goes without saying that it is a privilege to lead the prayers of a Christian community. But some people find it difficult both to stand up in front of others and to find some appropriate words. This small book is meant to be of practical help. It is meant to be a help in bringing context and coherence to community prayer. It could also be used for private prayer, of course, but that is not its main purpose.

The Alternative Service Book 1980 (page 124) provides for intercessions and thanksgivings to be led by the president of a Eucharist or by others. There are two forms where additional prayers or biddings can easily be inserted. One is in the main text of the Eucharist, the other is an alternative on page 166. In this book, they are shown separately. There is a third form, but it is a straightforward litany which requires equally straightforward use. It is printed on pages 67–9 below. Additionally, the Liturgical Commission of the Church of England has produced extra material in *Patterns of Worship* (published by Church House) and *The Promise of His Glory* (published by Church House and Mowbray). This is approved for use by the General Synod.

Originally, the ASB forms of intercession could be used with or without insertions. Not all paragraphs need to be used every time. But in my experience the concerns of a worshipping community are nearly always brought to this part of the service, and insertions, biddings, extempore prayer *are* used, together with the versicle 'Lord, in your mercy' and the response 'hear our prayer'.

This book suggests insertions and gives you a blank page at the end of each chapter so that you can write in your own favourite prayers. Please integrate the prayers I suggest in any way that your sensitivity dictates. Indeed, sensitivity, particularly to the balance of the service, is a key issue. The 'drive' and communicating power of the Eucharist can be ruined by endless prayers, by the use of jargon, by self-indulgent phrases like 'O Lord, I would just like to . . .'. Please keep a constant watch on which person of God the Holy Trinity you are addressing!

On pages 54–66, I have given you some prayers for use at the Festivals of the Church and for Special Occasions.

But now it might be as well to understand a little of what the prayer of intercession is about. All praying is like breathing — a natural activity — and yet it seems to create so much difficulty, so much guilt. It is simply the way to respond to God, the way to feed a day-to-day life so that, in the end, everyone can do something of what God wants. Christian prayer is quite firmly for those who decide to identify with the person of Jesus of Nazareth; it is for those who would change their lifestyle so that they bring their priorities into line with those of Jesus. Prayer is for those who would motivate themselves with the power that motivated Jesus.

So, if you have been given a 'hearty desire to pray' (or even less than a hearty desire — the position of most of us!), then you will be embarking on an adventure which has knowledge of God, love of God and the doing of God's will as an end result. Millions of people have discovered that this is the way to be alive. The whole purpose of Christian prayer is to deepen and intensify your humanity so that you may live, increasingly, a life of love — that is, a life invaded by God.

If prayer is a natural activity then there can be no more natural part of it than the desire to pray for others, for the world. After all, for people who care for the world the whole idea is attractive. There is a chance to *do* something. There is a chance of feeling less helpless when confronted by the suffering of the world. There is a chance of grasping an idea that seems so simple, so easily a facet of faith.

But beware. In my view, intercession is the most difficult form of prayer. It is shot through with dangers and misunderstandings. If it is a terrible wrong to manipulate people (and it is), how wrong is it to try to manipulate God and push him into doing what he does not want to do? Intercession is not magic. But that is precisely what it will be so long as we insist on wanting to use God as a power: a power to be used with approval when he does what we want, a power to be used against the physical laws of his universe. If we want guarantees of power, visible proof of God's work, then our understanding of religion is positively primeval.

Intercession is not to provide a divine warranty for the benefit of public relations — nor, incidentally, must *we* use intensive intercession to create a good public impression. I remember trying to fill Westminster Abbey with people praying for more and better priests. I thought that it would look good, and, after all, it might work. I was rebuked, sharply; and I deserved it. Intercession is not a short cut to save *us* from doing the work and achieving the results. So what is this prayer of intercession, rightly understood? Are the difficulties there to be overcome? Certainly, and to great benefit. The best picture of a right understanding of intercessionary prayer is a seemingly unrelated story at the beginning of chapter 2 of St Mark's Gospel. Because of the crowds, a paralysed man is lowered through a roof by four of his friends so that he lies in front of Jesus. The faith of the friends is commended and the paralysed man has his sins forgiven and his health restored. Real intercession is just this. It is bringing people and situations and laying them before Jesus. It is carrying people and situations and laying them before the love and the power of God in thanksgiving. And the most important message that the story can bring is that the sick man's friends had faith. Intercession *is* a matter of faith, not proof. Intercession is only conducted aright if it is believed that there is a harmony and a love at the heart of the universe which can be trusted.

'*If you abide in me and my words abide in you*, ask whatever you will and it shall be done for you' (John 15.7 RSV). What is important is to be, as St Paul would say, 'in Christ'. The person or the situation must be brought into all that Jesus has taught us about God and the lives we live in God's world. As Evelyn Underhill said, 'Real intercession is not merely a petition but a piece of work involving perfect, costly *self*-surrender to God for the work *he* wants done on other souls'. So the way of intercession (I use the word 'way' with real emphasis) for people is three-fold:

1. Offer your *own* faith and love and readiness to hold to God, come what may.
2. Offer your own faith that God is present in the world and in the life of the person to be prayed for.
3. Offer yourself as an instrument of God.

Follow this pattern with a list if you like. There is nothing wrong with having a list. It is not infantile, merely a record of those who have asked that your love should be shown in the way of prayer.

So much for people. What about situations? It can be difficult to hear the words 'Let us pray for Northern Ireland and for the Horn of Africa'. It is almost as if we want God to solve all the political and economic problems of these areas at a stroke. This is not the way God works. He works through people: it was Moses who led the people out of Egypt. And the very meaning of God in human form — in Jesus — is that God trusts *us*, and is willing to wait for us to trust him. Difficult, therefore, though it is to hold within ourselves all of Northern Ireland or the Horn of Africa, it need not matter. If the constant love of Christians all over the world is centred on Belfast or Addis Ababa, the fullness of God's presence is increased and he is brought nearer to all of us. And this is by the value of intercession in the Eucharist. Day and night by consecration, 'the bread and wine in the Eucharist assume an entirely different meaning from what they normally have. And the consecration of any wish, its being offered to God, will most certainly change its substance. We begin praying by thinking this is what I hope for in this situation and I trust God not to let me down; we end by thinking this is how the situation looks in the light of God's purpose, this is what I must now do to serve God in it, and this is what I really want' (J. Neville Ward, *The Use of Praying*, Epworth Press).

So, intercession involves *facing* why so many people do not receive what they *reasonably* want. The right stance is expressed by what a Jewish prisoner wrote on the wall of his prison in Cologne.

> I believe in the sun even when it is not shining.
> I believe in love, even when I cannot feel it.
> I believe in God, even when he is silent.

Colin Semper
Westminster Abbey, London SW1

Part 1
INTERCESSIONS
AT THE EUCHARIST

The usual form of Intercessions

STILLNESS

Churches can be noisy places these days. I discover that, before the schematized intercessions, it is sometimes wise to try and instil some stillness! There are two ways of doing this. The first is to say, firmly, 'Let us pray', and then to keep quiet for a while until the congregation settles to the task, the work. The other is to wait a moment, and then to use a prayer which has the power to command stillness — except to children. But they are part of the family and have every right to be there. Apart from using the first few verses of Psalm 139, here are two prayers which you might use. And please remember that you can keep silence *between* the sections.

We are silent before you, Lord, as we offer our lives in thanksgiving. Help us to be open, ready for when you speak in the stillness. Keep us relaxed both in body and mind, constant in our love towards you.

O God, let me rise to the edges of time and open my life to your eternity;
let me run to the edges of space and gaze into your immensity;
let me climb through the barriers of sound and pass into your silence;

and then, in stillness and silence, let me adore You,
Who are Life, Light, Love
without beginning and without end,
the Source, the Sustainer, the Restorer,
the Purifier of all that is.

Adapted from Sister Ruth SLG, *Oxford Book of Prayers*

The rubric on page 124 of The Alternative Service Book 1980 states: 'Intercessions and Thanksgivings are led by the president, or by others. The form below . . . or other suitable words, may be used.

'This form may be used (a) with the insertion of specific subjects between the paragraphs; (b) as a continuous whole with or without brief biddings.

'Not all paragraphs need be used on every occasion. Individual names may be added at the places indicated.

'This response may be used before or after each paragraph.'

Minister   Lord, in your mercy
All   **hear our prayer.**

THE CHURCH

Let us pray for the Church and for the world,
and let us thank God for his goodness.

Almighty God, our heavenly Father, you promised
through your Son Jesus Christ to hear us when we pray
in faith.

ASB

✗ Strengthen *N* our bishop and all your Church in the
service of Christ; that those who confess your name
may be united in your truth, live together in your love,
and reveal your glory in the world.

ASB

Introductory

Lord, we offer ourselves to you. Increase our faith
in your love, your goodness and your purpose. Enable
us to see you working in ourselves and in others.
Rescue us from cynicism so that we may grow and
flourish.

X Lord, everything we have, all that we are, comes from
you.
Our gifts, our talents, all our possibilities belong to us
only because they come direct from you. Help us not
to belittle these gifts of yours, not to bury them, but
rather use them to make you better known to the
people of our neighbourhood and to the people of the
world.

We are silent before you, Lord, as we offer our lives in
thanksgiving. Help us to be open, ready for when you
speak in the quiet. Keep us relaxed in both body and
mind, constant in our love towards you.

Renewal

O Risen Christ, whose wounds declare the suffering
and the victory of God; we thank you for bursting the
bonds of death.
Look at us now, look at *our* bonds, look at the things
which tie us down, which fasten our hands and hobble
our feet, which stop us from walking in your ways,
which stop us from doing your works, which tether us
so tightly to the dead weight of past failures.
As you have burst the bonds of death, so burst our
bonds and set us free.
Set us free from our pride, set us free from our sin.
Set us free from our fear, set us free from ourselves.
Stand in our midst. Lay on us your hands.
Breathe into us your breath.
So may the fire of your life fall upon us, that we may
have the faith to move mountains of irrelevance in our

churches, and may have the love without which faith is vain.
So give us speech that people may hear us speak in their own tongues.
So give us life that we may create an army of followers which can win the world for you.
Look at us Lord, and may this body be filled with your Spirit.
For your glory, for our peace, for the world and for your own name's sake.

James Jordan, broadcast on the BBC

Unity

Lord, in this service we feel our divisions. We are cut off from each other just at the moment when we should be together. We deliberately hurt you. Lord, break down the walls that separate us. Make it possible for your people to worship together in complete union and show us your way to bring it about.

Mission, Evangelism

Almighty God, you called us to your service to save us and keep us under your protection. Give your Church the love which knows no barriers of race or culture, and strengthen us with your trust so that we may accomplish your work in the world.

Lord, as we struggle to be faithful to you at a time when your claims are largely ignored or denied, we pray that we may bear our Christian witness by what we are and not simply by what we profess or preach. Give us holiness of character, a deeper understanding of our fellow human beings and their needs, and a love that is humble, outgoing and open. So may our lives reflect something of your grace.

Loosely based on words of George Appleton

Help us, Lord, to make sense of the gospel, and to relate it to the needs of others, so that they may be drawn to your love and worship and serve you in the family of the Church.

Adapted from the Cambridge Pastorate

Lord, I am two people; and one is filled with longing to serve you utterly, and one is afraid. Have compassion on me.
Lord, I am two people; and one will labour to the end, and one is weary already. Have compassion on me.
Lord, I am two people; and one knows the suffering of the world, and one knows only his/her [*use gender of leader*] own. Have compassion on me.
And may the spirit of freedom fill our hearts and the hearts of all people everywhere.

Adapted from a prayer used in St Martin-in-the-Fields

Reconciliation

Father, who formed our human family to live in
harmony and peace; we acknowledge before you our
divisions, quarrels, hatreds, injustices and greed.
May your Church demonstrate before the world the
power of the gospel to destroy divisions, so that in
your Son there may be no barriers of wealth or class,
age or intellect, race or colour but all may be equally
your children, members one of another and heirs
together of your everlasting Kingdom.

The Right Revd Timothy Dudley-Smith

Persecution

Lord, you know what it is to be despised and rejected
of men.
Be near to those who suffer because they believe in
you. Inspire them with your love and courage so that
others may be won to your perfect freedom.

Care

Lord, you have shown us that people who conquer all
by love are unconquerable. May we give ourselves for
the world and our fellow human beings, as you did
when you walked the earth. May those of us who are
the Church struggle to free those who are in any way
oppressed and restore to them the dignity of being
truly human.

Ministry

We thank you, O God, for our hunger and thirst for righteousness; our souls long for you, we respond to your call. Defend all those whose response to your call takes the form of service in the sacred ministry of your Church. Grant that your work may grow around them. Keep them in faith and in understanding of your will. Make their vision to be clear and their judgement to be sound. So may their journey be in enthusiasm, enjoyment and peace, shared with those they serve.

Your own prayers

THE WORLD

Bless and guide Elizabeth our Queen; give wisdom to
all in authority; and direct this and every nation in the
ways of justice and of peace; that men may honour one
another, and seek the common good.

ASB

Introductory

All the ends of the earth shall remember and turn to
the Lord, and all kindreds of the nations shall worship
before you. For the Kingdom is the Lord's and he is the
ruler over the nations.

Other Nations

We pray that we may settle our international differences
by wiser ways than war.
We pray that we may understand the needs and
aspirations of other nations.
We pray that we may respect the customs, traditions,
teachers and prophets of other cultures.
We pray that we may be filled with a spirit of goodwill
towards all people, and live together in peace.

Lord, give to the nations wisdom to understand the
things that belong to their peace and the will to reject

the things that make for war. And we pray that, realizing our common humanity, we may live together as a family and make the world a home, bearing one another's burdens, ministering to one another's needs, and obeying your laws in righteousness, as children of one God and Father.

George Appleton

Our Nation

God bless our land;
God guide our rulers;
God resolve our differences;
God revive our churches;
God forgive our selfishness;
God protect our homes;
God strengthen our faith.

The Right Revd Maurice Wood

Government

O Lord our God, we bring before you those who represent us in government. May they be channels of responsibility, integrity, wisdom and care so that through them your will may be done on earth as it is in heaven.

Justice

Lord, we pray for a truly prophetic understanding of our societies' difficulties, tensions and disorders. Stir in us a burning sense of justice and a true responsibility for one another. Enable us to create a loving community which is in total accord with your will.

The Social Services

We thank you, Lord, for all who work in the social services:
    for policemen and probation officers;
    for youth leaders and school teachers;
    for welfare officers and psychiatric social workers;
    for doctors, nurses and many others.
We pray that you will give to all such people sympathy and understanding, love and firmness.

Industry

Lord, we bring before you the industrial life of our nation and particularly those who work at *N* (and *N*) . . . within our community. Increase the understanding and co-operation of those who are engaged in a common purpose. Remove all tension, bitterness and prejudice so that all may strive together for what is just and wise and beneficial for the whole of humanity.

Peace

O God and Father of all, whom the whole heavens
adore; let the whole earth also worship you, all
kingdoms obey you, all tongues confess and bless you
and serve you in peace.

Adapted from *Prayers for Today*

The Arts

Spirit of God, creative inspiration of all that we do
which is beautiful and of good report, we thank you
for painting, sculpture, music, drama and literature
and all the endeavours which point us beyond
ourselves. We thank you for every enrichment of our
humanity and for the re-dedication which so naturally
follows.

The Media

Lord, you have entrusted to us the skills which enable
us to communicate with one another across the world.
We pray for those who influence the lives of others by
their writing or broadcasting. Give them a vision of a
world community where there is responsibility,
sensitivity to human need, and a real reverence for the
truth.

Your own prayers

THE LOCAL COMMUNITY

Give grace to us, our families and friends, and to all
our neighbours; that we may serve Christ in one
another, and love as he loves us.

ASB

The Family

Lord, you have experienced the pattern of family
life, and so we ask that our families may learn to
live together in love, respect and forgiveness. In
times of difficulty, strengthen us. In times of
perplexity, bring wisdom. In times of happiness,
make us thankful.

The Children

Give us the grace, Lord, to tell our children the truth
and nothing but the truth.
To issue no idle threats or promises.
To keep our word.
To apologize when we have been wrong.
To be disciplined over time.
To be courteous in all our dealings.
To answer children's questions as honestly and as
simply as we can.
To let them help in all the ways that we can devise.

To expect from them no higher standard of honesty, unselfishness, politeness than we are prepared to live up to ourselves.

Adapted from Joan Kendall

The Local Community

Lord God, you have made us members one of another; we are not strangers because we all seek the same homeland. We give you thanks that we have survived to this day in this local community. May your spirit invest our endeavours so that whatever contribution we make, it may be for the good of all. Prosper our thinking and our doing.

The Environment

Enlarge within us, O Lord, the sense of communion with all living things to whom you have given this earth as their home in common with us. We remember with shame that we have exercised our dominion of the earth with cruelty and irresponsibility. When our use of this world is over and we make room for others, may we not leave anything ravished by our greed or spoiled by our ignorance, but may we rather hand on our heritage fairer and sweeter through our use of it.

Adapted from *Hymns of the Social Awakening*

Schools, Colleges and Universities

Almighty God, you are truth and your spirit leads us into the truth: may all who teach and all who learn possess that integrity which alone can bring them knowledge of the truth. Let them never, for personal advantage, conceal the truth, nor, in pursuit of power, betray it. Let them never, for lack of courage, refuse to face the facts. Lead them to those depths of thought and discipline where you, O God, can make yourself known to them.

Adapted from *New Every Morning*

Your own prayers

THE TROUBLED

Comfort and heal all those who suffer in body,
mind, or spirit . . . ; give them courage and hope
in their troubles; and bring them the joy of your
salvation.

ASB

The Wounded World

Lord, you are love and you see all suffering, injustice
and misery. Have compassion upon the work of your
hands, the wounded world. Fill our hearts with love
for those who suffer. Help us to perceive the bond that
links Christian people with all mankind and which
helps in bearing one another's burdens.

The Sick

Lord, we carry into your presence those who are
sick in body or mind. We thank you for all your
work in those who struggle to restore them to good
health. Uphold our faith and the faith of those in
pain so that together we may trust and not be
afraid. May we all share in the task of making people
whole.

The Underprivileged

God of all beauty, whose will it is that all your
creatures should enjoy the world and the life you have
given us; we know that many are unable to do this
through hunger, poverty, disease, oppression,
ignorance or sin. Let us never rest content in your joys
until we have done everything in our power and by
your grace to help others to share them also. O God of
all goodness and willer of abundant life.

George Appleton

The Unemployed and the Homeless

Jesus, Son of Man, look in mercy upon all who suffer
the lack of livelihood and, like you, have nowhere to
lay their head; let your compassion move us to house
the homeless, that in you all the families of the earth
may be blessed.

Adapted from F. D. MacNutt

The Mentally Ill

Lord Jesus Christ, in the mystery of so much of mental
suffering, we look to you for an illumination that will
satisfy our hearts and minds. Your love for us took
you through great agony: encompass with that love all
who live in the darkness of mental illness, especially N.
You are the Light that has overcome darkness; pierce
the darkness to bring peace, unity and wholeness.

General

Lord, as we struggle to be faithful to you at a time
when your claims are largely ignored or denied, we
pray that we may bear our Christian witness by what
we are and not simply by what we profess or preach.
Give us holiness of character, a deeper understanding
of our fellow human beings and their needs, and a love
that is humble, outgoing and open. So may our lives
reflect something of your grace.

Loosely based on words of George Appleton

Help us, Lord, to make sense of the gospel, and to
relate it to the needs of others, so that they may be
drawn to your love and worship and serve you in the
family of the Church.

Adapted from the Cambridge Pastorate

Lord, I am two people; and one is filled with longing
to serve you utterly, and one is afraid. Have
compassion on me.
Lord, I am two people; and one will labour to the end,
and one is weary already. Have compassion on me.
Lord, I am two people; and one knows the suffering of
the world, and one knows only his/her [*use gender of
leader*] own. Have compassion on me.
And may the spirit of freedom fill our hearts and the
hearts of all people everywhere.

Adapted from a prayer used in St Martin-in-the-Fields

The Dying

We bring before you, O Lord Jesus Christ, those whose
earthly life is almost at an end. Lessen their fear,
encourage them on their journey and give them the
peace that comes from your victory over death.

Your own prayers

THE DEPARTED

Hear us as we remember those who have died in the faith of Christ . . . ; according to your promises, grant us with them a share in your eternal kingdom.

ASB

Those Who Have Died

In our mourning, Lord, we feel deprived of a vast treasure of human power, ability and goodness. We remember now those who have left a void in us and in our community. You have given us an assurance of eternal life by overcoming death. Help us now to take your promise seriously and to journey on our earthly pilgrimage with faith and constancy so that we may share with all your faithful servants the glory of a life which is eternal.

We thank you for the dear and faithful dead; for those who have made the distant heavens a home for us, and whose truth and beauty are even now in our hearts. One by one you gather the scattered families out of the earthly light into the heavenly glory, from the strife and distractions and weariness of time to the peace of eternity. We thank you for the labour and the joys of those mortal years and for our deep sense of the mysteries that lie beyond our dust. We thank you for

the eyes of faith which you have opened for all who
believe in your name.

Source unknown; given to me by Mrs Betty Tiarks at the time of the
death of her husband Geoffrey, my friend.

Communion of Saints

We thank you, O Lord our God, that the life which we
now live in Christ is part of the life which is eternal,
and the fellowship which we have in him unites us with
your whole Church on earth and in heaven; and we
pray that as we journey through the years we may
know joys which are without end, and at last come to
that abiding city where you reign for ever more.

New Every Morning

The Bereaved

O Jesus, whose compassion welled over into tears at
the death of friends. Enter the lives of those who
mourn their loved ones. From the heart which took
you to the Cross, bring them courage, faith and peace
in the immediate days to come.

Concluding Prayers

*These can be used before the final congregational
response:*
Grant, O Lord, that we may walk in your presence,
with your love in our hearts, your truth in our minds,
your strength in our wills; that when we finally stand
before you, it may be with the assurance of your
welcome and the joy of our homecoming.

Grant, O Lord, that we may lift our hearts to you in adoration. Our hunger is not for bread alone, but for your heavenly food. In the coming days, may our minds be fed by increasing knowledge of your word, may our inner lives be invaded by your holiness, may our imaginations be stimulated by your beauty, and may our wills be kept steadfast in your service.

Rejoicing in the fellowship of (*N* and of) all your saints, we commend ourselves and all Christian people to your unfailing love.

Merciful Father,
All accept these prayers
for the sake of your Son,
our Saviour Jesus Christ. Amen.

Your Own Prayers

The alternative form of Intercessions

STILLNESS

Churches can be noisy places these days. I discover that, before the schematized intercessions, it is sometimes wise to try and instil some stillness! There are two ways of doing this. The first is to say, firmly, 'Let us pray', and then keep quiet for a while until the congregation settles to the task, the work. The other is to wait a moment, and then to use a prayer which has the power to command stillness — except to children. But they are part of the family and have every right to be there. Apart from using the first few verses of Psalm 139, here are two prayers which you might use. And please remember that you can keep silence *between* the sections.

We are silent before you, Lord, as we offer our lives in thanksgiving. Help us to be open, ready for when you speak in the stillness. Keep us relaxed both in body and mind, constant in our love towards you.

O God, let me rise to the edges of time and open my life to your eternity;
let me run to the edges of space and gaze into your immensity;

let me climb through the barriers of sound and pass
into your silence;
and then, in stillness and silence, let me adore You,
Who are Life, Light, Love
without beginning and without end,
the Source, the Sustainer, the Restorer,
the Purifier of all that is.

Adapted from Sister Ruth SLG, *Oxford Book of Prayers*

At the end of each section the Minister says:

Lord, in your mercy
All   **hear our prayer.**

THE WORLD

Minister   Let us pray for the whole Church of God in
Christ Jesus, and for all men according to their
needs.

O God, the creator and preserver of all
mankind, we pray for men of every race,
and in every kind of need: make your ways
known on earth, your saving power among all
nations.

ASB

Introductory

All the ends of the earth shall remember and turn to
the Lord, and all kindreds of the nations shall worship
before you. For the Kingdom is the Lord's and he is the
ruler over the nations.

Other Nations

We pray that we may settle our international
differences by wiser ways than war.
We pray that we may understand the needs and
aspirations of other nations.
We pray that we may respect the customs,
traditions, teachers and prophets of other cultures.
We pray that we may be filled with a spirit of goodwill
towards all people, and live together in peace.

Lord, give to the nations wisdom to understand the
things that belong to their peace and the will to reject
the things that make for war. And we pray that,
realizing our common humanity, we may live together
as a family and make the world a home, bearing one
another's burdens, ministering to one another's needs,
and obeying your laws in righteousness, as children of
one God and Father.

George Appleton

The Social Services

We thank you, Lord, for all who work in the social
services:
  for policemen and probation officers;
  for youth leaders and school teachers;
  for welfare officers and psychiatric social workers;
  for doctors, nurses and many others.
We pray that you will give to all such people sympathy
and understanding, love and firmness.

Industry

Lord, we bring before you the industrial life of our nation and particularly those who work at *N* (and *N*) . . . within our community. Increase the understanding and co-operation of those who are engaged in a common purpose. Remove all tension, bitterness and prejudice so that all may strive together for what is just and wise and beneficial for the whole of humanity.

Peace

O God and Father of all, whom the whole heavens adore; let the whole earth also worship you, all kingdoms obey you, all tongues confess and bless you, and serve you in peace.

Adapted from *Prayers for Today*

The Arts

Spirit of God, creative inspiration of all that we do which is beautiful and of good report, we thank you for painting, sculpture, music, drama and literature and all the endeavours which point us beyond ourselves. We thank you for every enrichment of our humanity and for the re-dedication which so naturally follows.

The Media

Lord, you have entrusted to us the skills which enable
us to communicate with one another across the world.
We pray for those who influence the lives of others by
their writing or broadcasting. Give them a vision of
a world community where there is responsibility,
sensitivity to human need, and a real reverence for the
truth.

Minister	Lord, in your mercy
All	**hear our prayer.**

Your own prayers

THE CHURCH

Minister   We pray for your Church throughout the
world: guide and govern us by your Holy
Spirit, that all who profess and call
themselves Christians may be led into the
way of truth, and hold the faith in unity
of spirit, in the bond of peace, and in
righteousness of life.

ASB

Introductory

Lord, we offer ourselves to you. Increase our faith
in your love, your goodness and your purpose. Enable
us to see you working in ourselves and in others.
Rescue us from cynicism so that we may grow and
flourish.

Lord, everything we have, all that we are, comes from
you.
Our gifts, our talents, all our possibilities belong to us
only because they come direct from you. Help us not
to belittle these gifts of yours, not to bury them, but
rather use them to make you better known to the
people of our neighbourhood and to the people of the
world.

We are silent before you, Lord, as we offer our lives in thanksgiving. Help us to be open, ready for when you speak in the quiet. Keep us relaxed in both body and mind, constant in our love towards you.

Renewal

O Risen Christ, whose wounds declare the suffering and the victory of God; we thank you for bursting the bonds of death.
Look at us now, look at *our* bonds, look at the things which tie us down, which fasten our hands and hobble our feet, which stop us from walking in your ways, which stop us from doing your works, which tether us so tightly to the dead weight of past failures.
As you have burst the bonds of death, so burst our bonds and set us free.
Set us free from our pride, set us free from our sin.
Set us free from our fear, set us free from ourselves.
Stand in our midst. Lay on us your hands.
Breathe into us your breath.
So may the fire of your life fall upon us, that we may have the faith to move mountains of irrelevance in our churches, and may have the love without which faith is vain.
So give us speech that people may hear us speak in their own tongues.
So give us life that we may create an army of followers which can win the world for you.
Look at us Lord, and may this body be filled with your Spirit.

For your glory, for our peace, for the world and for
your own name's sake.

James Jordan, broadcast on the BBC

Unity

Lord, in this service we feel our divisions. We are cut
off from each other just at the moment when we
should be together. We deliberately hurt you. Lord,
break down the walls that separate us. Make it possible
for your people to worship together in complete union
and show us your way to bring it about.

Mission, Evangelism

Almighty God, you called us to your service to save us
and keep us under your protection. Give your Church
the love which knows no barriers of race or culture,
and strengthen us with your trust so that we may
accomplish your work in the world.

Lord, as we struggle to be faithful to you at a time
when your claims are largely ignored or denied, we
pray that we may bear our Christian witness by what
we are and not simply by what we profess or preach.
Give us holiness of character, a deeper understanding
of our fellow human beings and their needs, and a love
that is humble, outgoing and open. So may our lives
reflect something of your grace.

Loosely based on words of George Appleton

Help us, Lord, to make sense of the gospel, and to relate it to the needs of others, so that they may be drawn to your love and worship and serve you in the family of the Church.

Adapted from the Cambridge Pastorate

Lord, I am two people; and one is filled with longing to serve you utterly, and one is afraid. Have compassion on me.
Lord, I am two people; and one will labour to the end, and one is weary already. Have compassion on me.
Lord, I am two people; and one knows the suffering of the world, and one knows only his/her [*use gender of leader*] own. Have compassion on me.
And may the spirit of freedom fill our hearts and the hearts of all people everywhere.

Adapted from a prayer used in St Martin-in-the-Fields

Reconciliation

Father, who formed our human family to live in harmony and peace; we acknowledge before you our divisions, quarrels, hatreds, injustices and greed. May your Church demonstrate before the world the power of the gospel to destroy divisions, so that in your Son there may be no barriers of wealth or class, age or intellect, race or colour but all may be equally your children, members one of another and heirs together of your everlasting Kingdom.

The Right Revd Timothy Dudley-Smith

Persecution

Lord, you know what it is to be despised and rejected
of men.
Be near to those who suffer because they believe in
you. Inspire them with your love and courage so that
others may be won to your perfect freedom.

Care

Lord, you have shown us that people who conquer all
by love are unconquerable. May we give ourselves for
the world and our fellow human beings, as you did
when you walked the earth. May those of us who are
the Church struggle to free those who are in any way
oppressed and restore to them the dignity of being
truly human.

Ministry

We thank you, O Lord, for our hunger and thirst for
righteousness; our souls long for you, we respond to
your call. Defend all those whose response to your call
takes the form of service in the sacred ministry of your
Church. Grant that your work may grow around them.
Keep them in faith and in understanding of your will.
Make their vision to be clear and their judgement to be
sound. So may their journey be in enthusiasm,
enjoyment and peace, shared with those they serve.

     Lord, in your mercy
All   hear our prayer.

Your own prayers

THE TROUBLED

Minister   We commend to your fatherly goodness all
who are anxious or distressed in mind or
body; comfort and relieve them in their need;
give them patience in their sufferings, and
bring good out of their troubles.

ASB

The Wounded World

Lord, you are love and you see all suffering, injustice
and misery. Have compassion upon the work of your
hands, the wounded world. Fill our hearts with love
for those who suffer. Help us to perceive the bond that
links Christian people with all mankind and which
helps in bearing one another's burdens.

The Sick

Lord, we carry into your presence those who are sick
in body and mind. We thank you for all your work in
those who struggle to restore them to good health.
Uphold our faith and the faith of those in pain so that
together we may trust and not be afraid. May we all
share in the task of making people whole.

The Underprivileged

God of all beauty, whose will it is that all your
creatures should enjoy the world and the life you have
given us; we know that many are unable to do this
through hunger, poverty, disease, oppression,
ignorance or sin. Let us never rest content in your joys
until we have done everything in our power and by
your grace to help others to share them also. O God of
all goodness and willer of abundant life.

George Appleton

The Unemployed and the Homeless

Jesus, Son of Man, look in mercy upon all who suffer
the lack of livelihood and, like you, have nowhere to
lay their head; let your compassion move us to house
the homeless, that in you all the families of the earth
may be blessed.

Adapted from F. D. MacNutt

The Mentally Ill

Lord Jesus Christ, in the mystery of so much of mental
suffering, we look to you for an illumination that will
satisfy our hearts and minds. Your love for us took
you through great agony: encompass with that love all
who live in the darkness of mental illness, especially *N*.
You are the Light that has overcome darkness; pierce
the darkness to bring peace, unity and wholeness.

The Dying

We bring before you, O Lord Jesus Christ, those whose
earthly life is almost at an end. Lessen their fear,
encourage them on their journey and give them the
peace that comes from your victory over death.

At the end the Minister says:

Merciful Father,
All **accept these prayers**
for the sake of your Son,
our Saviour Jesus Christ. Amen.

Your own prayers

The Festivals of the Church and Special Occasions

Advent

Lord God, we are preparing to celebrate the birth of your Son Jesus Christ. While we recall his coming as a child, in weakness and humility, may we be reminded that one day he will come in power and glory. In this season of Advent, may we find time to reflect on the wonder of your love and allow the story of the birth of Christ to penetrate our hearts and wills. So may our joy be deeper, our worship more real, and our lives more worthy.

Adapted from the *Catholic Prayer Book* and Frank Colquhoun

Christmas

Before the main prayers:

While all things were in silence, and night was in the midst of her swift course, your Almighty Word, O Lord, leaped down out of your royal throne. Alleluia.

Adapted from Christmas Vespers, Western Rite

Lord God, when you wanted to speak to us in a language we would understand, Christ the Word came. When you wanted to weld yourself and your world

together, Christ the Lord came. When you wanted to
show your trust in human flesh, Christ the Child came.
With all our heart and with all our mind we thank you
for this profound mystery of Christmas, by which our
lives are changed.

New Year

Lord, our help in ages past, our hope for years to
come, we ask that you will take our lives under your
protection for the next part of our journey. May your
wisdom direct us, your power defend us, and your love
enfold us.

Epiphany

Almighty and everlasting God, who by the guidance of
a star led the wise men to fall before the new-born
King in adoration,
    we praise you that the light of Christ shines amidst
the darkness of the world
    we praise you for the good news he came to bring to
all the people
    we praise you for the whole Christian family,
worshipping and bearing witness to him.
Receive, O Lord Christ, these our praises and fill the
world with the radiance of your glory.

Ash Wednesday

Lord, feed our souls that we may continually live in you and you in us. Purify us in our obedience. Protect us in temptation. Renew our spirits with your endless life. So may we follow you to your Cross in greater holiness and love.

Mothering Sunday

Lord Christ, receive our thanks for those who have nurtured us from our earliest years. Hear our prayer for mothers everywhere, for all that they are and all that they do. May we honour them, not take them for granted. And may the signs of your kingdom be unfolded in the lives of our families, the signs of justice, peace, growth and love.

Passiontide

Lord Christ, who entered into your triumph by the hard and lonely way of the Cross; may your courage and integrity, and your unswerving devotion to the Father's will, inspire us to walk firmly and with joy the path which love bids us take, even though it may lead us through suffering, misunderstanding and darkness. We ask this for your sake who, for the joy that was set before you, endured the Cross, despising the shame, and are now seated at the right hand of the throne of God the Father.

Adapted from *With All Our Strength*

Palm Sunday

Lord, on this Palm Sunday you were given a hero's welcome, but you chose to demonstrate power in the grip of humility. Empty our lives of all vain strength so that we may follow in your steps on the journey that you have chosen for us, and shown to us.

Maundy Thursday

Before the main prayers:

The Master shows to his followers an example of humility. He who wraps the heaven in clouds girds himself with a towel; and he in whose hand is the life of all things kneels down to wash the feet of his servants.

From Matins, Orthodox Church

Lord, you gave us this memorial of your suffering until the end of time; feed us with yourself in bread and wine, strengthen us in holiness, that this family may live in the struggle of faith and in one communion of love.

Good Friday

Lord Christ, as we draw near to you this day under the shadow of your Cross; give us a new understanding of your sorrow over us, true repentance for our sins for which you suffered, and an even deeper gratitude for your rescuing love for us and all people, everywhere.

Easter

Before the main prayers:

May the light of Christ, rising in glory, scatter the
darkness of our heart and mind. Alleluia.

From the Blessing of the New Fire, Roman Missal

or

Praise be to the God and Father of our Lord Jesus
Christ! In his great mercy he has given us new birth
and living hope by raising Jesus Christ from the dead,
and the promise of a heavenly inheritance which can
never be spoilt or soiled or wither away. Trusting in
him we obtain the salvation of our souls and rejoice
with unutterable and exalted joy. Alleluia.

Based on 1 Peter 1.3–9

Lord our God, as we celebrate with joy the resurrection
of Jesus, help us to make the Easter faith a deeper
reality in our lives; that we may know something more
of the peace he bequeathed to his followers and lay
hold of the victory he won for us over sin and
tribulation and death, rejoicing in the hope of the life
immortal which is ours in him, our rescuer and our
Lord.

Adapted from Frank Colquhoun

Rogation

(See The Environment on page 25)

Almighty Father, by whose blessing the earth brings
forth abundantly all that is needful for our lives;
prosper the work of farmers and all those engaged in
the production of our daily bread, that with thankful
hearts they may reap the fruit of their labour and that
we may rejoice in your great goodness.

Adapted from *New Every Morning*

Almighty God, you have graciously given us this world
to live in; may we respect both natural law and the law
of your Spirit; that in using and, above all, sharing this
world's resources we may be made fit for the whole
company of heaven.

Ascension

Before the main prayers:

Christ is the King to whom all authority has been given
in heaven and on earth. We own him as our Lord. We
yield him our obedience. We dedicate our lives to his
service. Come, Lord Christ, and reign in us, and make
us agents of your kingdom in the world. Alleluia.

Frank Colquhoun

Almighty God, we give you praise because you have exalted your Son to your right hand and bestowed on him the name above all names, that at the name of Jesus every knee should bow.

Wherefore, O God, accept our homage, our adoration, our thanksgiving; and grant that we may confess that Jesus Christ is Lord.

Based on Philippians 2.5-11

Pentecost/Whitsuntide

Before the main prayer:

The Holy Spirit is light and life, a living fountain of knowledge. The Holy Spirit is wisdom and understanding, loving, righteous, full of power. Alleluia.

Adapted from Vespers of Pentecost, Orthodox Church

Spirit of truth, Comforter, you are everywhere and you fill all things. You are the treasury of all good, you are the giver of life itself. Come and live within us. Take from our lives all that denies inspiration. Challenge us. Refresh us. With your power, grant us the nerve and the vision to accomplish what you would have us do.

Trinity Sunday

Before the main prayer:

Let us give praise to the Father who by his grace has adopted us as children

Let us give praise to the Son who by his death and rising has brought us new life

Let us give praise to the Spirit who dwells within us and inspires us for service

To the Holy and blessed Trinity be praise for ever.

Grant to us, O Holy Trinity, to worship in spirit and in truth, to submit all our natures to you; that our consciences may be quickened by your holiness, our minds nourished by your truth, our imaginations purified by your beauty. Help us to open our hearts to your love, and to surrender our wills to your purpose. O God, your immensity fills the earth and the whole universe, but the universe cannot contain you, much less the earth, and still less the world of our thoughts.

Based on words by George Appleton and Yves Raguin

Harvest Thanksgiving

Almighty God, we are taught by your word that for our daily needs we are dependent not only on the work of our hands, but also on your providence. We give you thanks at this time for your gifts to us in nature by which the earth is enriched and made fruitful, and for the labours of those by whom the harvest is gathered in. Instil a thankful heart in us for all that we receive, and enable us the more to understand that we are workers together with you, the author and giver of all good things.

Adapted from Frank Colquhoun

Remembrance

Before the main prayers:

In memory of those who have died in the wars of our time, we commit ourselves to be doers of peace. And we pray for peace in our hearts, in our homes, in our nations, in our world: the peace of your will, the peace of our need.

Based on words by George Appleton

Almighty God, we remember with thanksgiving those who died for us in the wars of our time. We pray that the offering of their lives may not have been in vain. Enable us this day to dedicate ourselves again to the cause of justice, freedom and peace. Give us the strength to build a better world.

A Saint's (or Saints') Day

We thank you, O God, for the saints of all ages, especially your servant(s) *N* (and *N*). For all those who in times of darkness kept the lamp of faith burning; for the great souls who saw visions of a larger truth and dared to declare it; for the multitude of quiet and gracious people whose presence has purified the world and made it holy; and for those known and loved by us who have passed from communion with us into the fuller communion of life with you.

Ember Days

For the ministry of the Church:

Raise up, O God, for the work of your Church men and
women of spiritual maturity and strong faith, men and
women of wide vision and sound judgement, and
above all men and women with a deep love for their
Lord and for their fellow human beings; that your
Church may be served in days to come by those whose
lives are wholly dedicated to the furtherance of your
Kingdom.

Based on words by Frank Colquhoun

Local Government

Lord God, we pray for those who are given authority
and responsibility among us in the work of the Council
(or County, or . . .); in administering the law and
maintaining peace, in education and the care of children,
in planning and building, in care for the disadvantaged,
in providing both for work and for leisure.

Direct and use their influence, that together we may
build a community whose life does honour to your
name and the vision of your Kingdom.

Human Rights

Lord God, in your Kingdom the walls that separate us
are broken down because all of us are created in your
image; grant us fearlessly to contend against abuses of
human rights. May we struggle to create a world where
people reverently use their freedom in the maintenance
of justice, in thought and in speech, and in worship of
you.

Education Sunday

Lord, the goal of all knowledge and the source of all truth; you lead us towards yourself along the paths of discovery and learning. Direct the work of education so that all good learning may flourish and abound. May your spirit of adventure and wisdom inspire all who teach and all who learn so that we may gain greater understanding of your purposes for all people.

Hospital Sunday

Lord of love, giver of life and health; we pray for all who in their various callings serve the needs of men and women in sickness of body or mind, especially in N (and N) Hospital(s). Equip them as your fellow workers in the ministry of healing and strengthen them to share in the task of making life whole.

Adapted from Basil Naylor

Sea Sunday

Lord, we pray for all seafarers as they fulfil their duties and face the dangers of their work:
>   the members of the Royal Navy and Merchant Navy;
>   the keepers of lighthouses, lightships, weatherships;
>   the pilots of our ports;
>   all who carry out the services of docks and harbours;
>   those who operate lifeboats and guard our coasts.
Grant them your strength and protection, and keep them in the hour of special need.

Patronal, Dedication Festival

Before the main prayers;

No one entering a house ignores those who live there.
This is the house of God and he is here. Pray to him
who loves you and bids you welcome. Give thanks for
those who in years past built this place to his glory.
Rejoice in his gifts of beauty in art and music,
architecture and handicraft, and worship him, the God
and Father of us all.

Baptism at the Eucharist

Keep us mindful, O Lord our God, that when we were
baptized into union with Christ, we were baptized into
his death that we might die to sin. We pray that as
Christ was raised from the dead by your glorious
power, so we may now walk in newness of life as those
who are no longer under the dominion of sin and
death.

Confirmation — First Communion

Almighty God, we thank you for those who in
confirmation have made their confession of faith in
you. We welcome them into the communicant life of
the Christian family in this church. May we, by our
friendship, our prayers and our example encourage
them in the way of Christ, that they may grow ever
nearer to the stature of him and continue steadfastly in
the worship and life of the Church.

Adapted from Frank Colquhoun

Marriage at the Family Eucharist

We carry into your presence, Almighty Father, *N* and *M*. May their marriage be for them a source of great and lasting joy. Spare them long to each other, and keep them faithful, tender and true, so that they may live together with deep happiness and peace. May your blessing be upon their home and in all the work that they do.

Adapted from *Worship Now*

Stewardship

Almighty God, your Son, though he was rich, yet for our sakes became poor, that we through his poverty might become rich; grant us the spirit of generous self-giving that we might further the work of this Christian community and relieve those who are in need. Help us who have so freely received from you to give as freely in return, and so share the blessedness of giving as well as the happiness of receiving.

Adapted from George Appleton

A Litany

Minister	In the power of the Spirit and in union with Christ, let us pray to the Father.
	Hear our prayers, O Lord our God.
All	**Hear us, good Lord.**
Minister	Govern and direct your holy Church; fill it with love and truth; and grant it that unity which is your will.
All	**Hear us, good Lord.**
Minister	Give us boldness to preach the gospel in all the world, and to make disciples of all the nations.
All	**Hear us, good Lord.**
Minister	Enlighten your ministers with knowledge and understanding, that by their teaching and their lives they may proclaim your word.
All	**Hear us, good Lord.**
Minister	Give your people grace to hear and receive your word, and to bring forth the fruit of the Spirit.
All	**Hear us, good Lord.**
Minister	Bring into the way of truth all who have erred and are deceived.
All	**Hear us, good Lord.**

Minister	Strengthen those who stand; comfort and help the faint-hearted; raise up the fallen; and finally beat down Satan under our feet.
All	**Hear us, good Lord.**
Minister	Guide the leaders of the nations into the ways of peace and justice.
All	**Hear us, good Lord.**
Minister	Guard and strengthen your servant Elizabeth our Queen, that she may put her trust in you, and seek your honour and glory.
All	**Hear us, good Lord.**
Minister	Endue the High Court of Parliament and all the Ministers of the Crown with wisdom and understanding.
All	**Hear us, good Lord.**
Minister	Bless those who administer the law, that they may uphold justice, honesty, and truth.
All	**Hear us, good Lord.**
Minister	Teach us to use the fruits of the earth to your glory, and for the good of all mankind.
All	**Hear us, good Lord.**
Minister	Bless and keep all your people.
All	**Hear us, good Lord.**
Minister	Help and comfort the lonely, the bereaved, and the oppressed.
All	**Lord, have mercy.**
Minister	Keep in safety those who travel, and all who are in danger.
All	**Lord, have mercy.**

Minister	Heal the sick in body and mind, and provide for the homeless, the hungry, and the destitute.
All	**Lord, have mercy.**
Minister	Show your pity on prisoners and refugees, and all who are in trouble.
All	**Lord, have mercy.**
Minister	Forgive our enemies, persecutors, and slanderers, and turn their hearts.
All	**Lord, have mercy.**
Minister	Hear us as we remember those who have died in the peace of Christ, both those who have confessed the faith and those whose faith is known to you alone, and grant us with them a share in your eternal kingdom.
All	**Lord, have mercy.**
Minister	Father, you hear those who pray in the name of your Son; grant that what we have asked in faith we may obtain according to your will; through Jesus Christ our Lord. **Amen.**

Part 2
INTERCESSIONS AT MORNING AND EVENING PRAYER

You will have noticed that I have pointed mainly to brief, cogent, collect-style prayers as the substantial cement to the intercessions at the Eucharist. This is because I believe firmly that the Eucharist is a drama in several acts, and, like any drama, it needs 'drive' to make its full impact. To pursue the image, the motor of the Eucharist may well travel in several gears, but it is hardly ever idling in neutral; the motor is under power. For example, there is the power of participation in music and prayer, the power of attention to the readings, the power of pilgrimage to receive bread and wine.

In Morning and Evening Prayer, Matins and Evensong, there is more space, a little bit of spiritual elbow-room. This does not mean that care and discipline vanish away but rather that different approaches can be tried.

WHEN TO USE INTERCESSIONS

In those churches which have used the Book of Common Prayer — or a service close to it — it has become the custom to have a time for prayer which is isolated between, say, an anthem or a hymn, and very firmly after the Office of Morning or Evening Prayer. But where the ASB is used, the intercessions can precede or follow the Lord's Prayer. In this case, the set prayers should not be used; they are not obligatory anyway.

SILENCE

The ASB provides for silence, and the offers need to be taken up. For example, it is suggested that silence follows the readings. And silence *does* follow the readings these days in many churches. However, a curious custom has grown up that the reader says 'Here ends the lesson', and *then* there is silence. The intention of the compilers is that the silent reflection follows the lesson, feeds off the lesson, and only ends when the officiant continues.

But silence must almost *always* be a part of the prayers, quite simply because people demand it. And people are right; there are so few opportunities for concentrated, attentive silence these days.

POSTURE

The Christian community ought to encourage itself towards silence — and towards good posture. You may think that I am being too scrupulous for words. But I am not. Many instructions in orders of service say 'Please kneel or sit for the prayers'. If you sit (I do), sit attentively with a straight back and still hands and head. As a great spiritual teacher said, if you are 'sloppy' on the outside, you will be 'sloppy' on the inside!

PREPARATION

If you are going to lead intercessions or a passage of prayer during a service, you will need to prepare. You will need to think about the theme which will normally complement the theme of the whole service. Themes are a great aid to communication. Everything — hymns, prayers, readings, address, music, silence — carries the theme along. So the prayers need to fit into the overall pattern and also add a step or two to the progression of the theme. It is very inspiring to be swept along by a great theme which has been simply and intelligently thought out. So it is not a bad idea to draw a few consecutive rectangular boxes and write a single word or phrase which will carry the subjects for prayer and show the delivery or enhancement of the theme. But someone will say that this is too clinical and leaves no room for spontaneity, the movement of the spirit and so on. I do not believe this. Any master of improvisation on a musical instrument will tell you that it emerges from great knowledge, technique and practice. In other words, more perspiration than inspiration. It is so with prayer. Prayer is a struggle. The exception *might* be when there is *no* leader of the prayers, *no* preparation, and the community of believers takes over the time in freedom and ecstasy of heart and utterance. I have sometimes been impressed by this but not often.

The Quaker way is hugely impressive but comes, of course, from deep silence, reflection, discipline and study. In Quaker Meetings I have attended there has not been much self-indulgence. If there were, it would be pared away (to put it mildly) by the Meeting. I have been enlivened by the Pentecostal or charismatic traditions, but I personally have not been much fed. I have listened for prophetic utterance but have only ever heard banal thought couched in tortuous Elizabethan English. It is fine for personal edification, as St Paul says. It is fine if it is religion of the heart. But if it degenerates into self-indulgence or, even worse, manipulation, then it is sinful.

I have several times heard at such gatherings: 'Father God, we have prayed and you have told us that someone here has AIDS and needs to tell us about it . . .' or 'is burdened by some heavy sin'. This is disrespectful of humanity. On the whole, even so-called 'free prayer' needs the light hand of a respected leader of the Christian community on the tiller. And lest you should think otherwise, I am much in favour of 'free prayer', provided that it is humble, thoughtful and compassionate.

SOME WAYS WITH INTERCESSIONS IN CHURCH

THE BIDDINGS

The leader speaks a couple of sentences, there is, perhaps, a short silence, and then a short verse and response, e.g.

Leader   Lord in your mercy
All   **Hear our prayer.**

This seems very simple and easily compiled. It is not. If you hear a fine exponent and a poor exponent, you will agree with me. It is very much the art that conceals art. I have a colleague at Westminster Abbey who, on his day, practises this art in a way which reaches to the sublime. He speaks a couple of sentences which suggest the subject of the fugue. Then — in a second bidding — he suggests another subject which develops the first and takes it on a bit. And somehow he incorporates what ought to be there, e.g. prayers for the Church, the world, the local and national community, the sick, the departed, in such a way that the head is gently engaged, the heart and will more fully engaged and the spirit enlivened at being led into the *divine* life. It *is* an art, an art not given the credit it deserves — like poetry.

Draw your rectangular, consecutive boxes, reflect deeply on the theme, pick up your pen, write — and mix with silence and a simple short verse and response. Beware of going on too long. It is an intense way of praying, and, like reality, humankind cannot bear too much intensity. Here is an attempt. The theme of the service has been 'The Venture of Faith'.

Faith is a way of believing, trusting, seeing that beneath what we *can* see there is vastly more that we *cannot* see.

Silence

Leader   Lord, that we may receive our sight.
All   **Amen.**

Faith is a way of looking at the world and believing that, despite the evidence to the contrary, God is in control.

Silence

Leader   Lord, that we may see the Father.
All   **Amen.**

When things of love and light happen, faith clings on to them for dear life. Because that is what they are.

Silence

Leader   Lord, that our faith may change even just a
             little suffering into light and love.
All   **Amen.**

Faith is waiting for the word of God which heals the wounds of history, illuminates the present, and opens the future.

Silence

Leader	Lord, our souls wait for you, and in your word is our trust.
All	**Amen.**

Faith lets the future approach. It creates the future from the present. It wrestles with the present to gain from it a blessing for the future.

Silence

Leader	It is you, Lord, we will not be afraid.
All	**Amen.**

Faith is more faith-ful when it is tempted and threatened. In the face of every misgiving and reserve, it continues to say 'My Lord and my God'.

Silence

Leader	Lord, I believe, help my unbelief.
All	**Amen.**

Faith is to participate in the way of Jesus, to share in the power that motivated him, to share in the power that raised him from the dead. Faith is not the precondition of salvation, but the assurance of it.

Silence

Leader	Lord, I will give thanks to you for ever.
All	**Amen.**

A litany is not very different from what I have written about biddings. Perhaps it is a bit more prosaic, and none the worse for that, because it is more kaleidoscopic. I am not suggesting here a largesse of litanies; you can discover them for yourselves. The best collection I know is in Jeffrey W. Rowthorn, *The Wideness of God's Mercy — Litanies to Enlarge our Prayer* (2 volumes; The Seabury Press). There is a litany for every conceivable occasion or theme. Here, as an example of decent quality (like everything he did), is a Litany for All Workers by Reinhold Niebuhr.

O God, you have made us a royal priesthood, that we might offer to you prayer and intercession for people of every sort and condition; hear us as we pray.

For all who toil in the burden and heat of the day, that they may enjoy the rewards of their industry, that they may not be defrauded of their due, and that we may never cease to be mindful of our debt to them, remembering with gratitude the multitude of services which must be performed to make our life tolerable:

We pray your grace and pledge our concern, O God.

For those who have authority and power over their fellows, that they may not use it for selfish advantage, but be guided to do justice and to love mercy:

We pray your grace and pledge our concern, O God.

For those who have been wounded in the battles of life, whether by the inhumanity of their fellows, their own limitations, or the fickleness of fortune, that they may contend against injustice without bitterness, overcome their own weakness with diligence, and learn how to accept with patience what cannot be altered.

We pray your grace and pledge our concern, O God.

For the rulers of the nations, that they may act wisely and without pride, may seek to promote peace among the peoples, and establish justice in our common life:

We pray your grace and pledge our concern, O God.

For teachers and ministers of the Word, for artists and interpreters of our spiritual life, that they may rightly divine the word of truth, and not be tempted by pride or greed or any ignoble passion to corrupt the truth to which they are committed:

We pray your grace and pledge our concern, O God.

For prophets and seers and saints, who awaken us from our sloth, that they may continue to hold their torches high in a world darkened by prejudice and sin, and ever be obedient to the heavenly vision:

We pray your grace and pledge our concern, O God.

O Lord, you have bound us together in this bundle of life, give us grace to understand how our lives depend upon the courage, the industry, the honesty and integrity of our fellows; that we may be mindful of their needs, grateful for their faithfulness, and faithful in our responsibilities to them; through Jesus Christ our Lord.

Amen.

You can buy books of specialist litanies. For example, there is a compilation by Cameron Butland on the world of work. Entitled *Work in Worship*, it is published by Hodder & Stoughton for the Industrial Christian Fellowship. If you worship in an urban Christian community there would be much of general relevance in this book.

FREE PRAYER

There are three main ways of using free prayer. The first is for the worship leader to say 'And now a time of prayer', and leave it entirely to the community.

The second is to indicate a time of free prayer within a more structured offering, for example, when it comes to praying for the sick, the frail, the house-bound, the troubled, the dying, the departed.

The third is for the worship leader to suggest the theme or repeat the theme and leave it to the members of the community to expand it, illuminate it, shape it, personalize it, in prayer.

I repeat: be aware of the dangers but also be aware of the huge advantages for growth in the Christian life if either the leadership is sensitive or people are sensitive to one another in the Christian community. Exhibitionism, prejudice, the utterance of the latest pet mini-sermon — these are the things which give free prayer the bad name that it should never have.

FREE PRAYER IN SILENCE

This requires much teaching and much use for it to mean anything to the broader Christian community. It takes a huge amount of time to get right. The way to start is in a community prayer group which must *always* be attended by the acknowledged Christian leader, for example, the parish priest. Patient teaching about contemplation for today is followed by ever-lengthening silence. Start with fifteen minutes and treble it over the months. Sometimes it is right for the leader to offer a subject for meditation, and sometimes it is right for people to drop their prayers or insights into the pool of silence. If the Christian leader supports this kind of prayer, at first people will come, and then most of them, in my experience, will fall away. The core that is left is the most important brick in any Christian community. It is possible that this core can affect the general, Sunday worship. If so, it is the pearl of great price. But the pearl is not to be had for nothing and so is very rare. Just occasionally I have encountered a group of still, conscious, mindful, collected people; and they have the precious gift of turning this way and that and yet they never move. It is because they have touched the stillness at the heart of things.

THE TIME OF PRAYER

This is a time given over to various elements of prayer. It is a constructed time, the various elements pointing to the theme. Music, poetry, collects, readings from the Bible and other writings all follow one upon another in a sort of prayer anthology. Because they are sung and spoken, they must be plainly constructed; there is no chance to turn back the page and read it all again. So, when one item is immediately followed by another, the second item must amplify or expound the first and take it on further. There has to be an element of 'tell them what they *will* hear, tell them, and then tell them what they have heard'. It sounds simplistic but it is not. If the participant is not obviously led, then the value is diminished. This anthological approach takes a bit more time and is perhaps more suitable in acts of worship where there is no address; it is also suitable on great festivals when the theme is (we hope) abundantly obvious. The principle is always: keep it simple. If you think that if you keep it simple it will not be profound, you should not be doing it.

Here is an example for Harvest Thanksgiving. It has a popular hymn as the spine and needs a cantor, a musical instrument, and a few people prepared to walk with gifts to a prominent table.

Leader   Let us with gladness present the offerings of our life and work to the Lord.

Cantor sings first and then everyone:

> Let us with a gladsome mind
> Praise the Lord for he is kind.
> For his mercies aye endure
> Ever faithful, ever sure.

The musical instrument continues to play, quietly, as a member of the community walks to the table with a loaf of bread. With voice over music the leader says:

> The gift of bread.
>
> The eyes of all wait upon you, O God.

All   **And you give them their food in due season.**

Member   I present to God, on behalf of all of us, this bread, the staff of life. It is a token of our gratitude that he sends all things needful for

our souls and bodies. So I ask us to pray
for those whose daily work provides our
food and clothing, those who work on land
and sea. I ask us to thank God for this
community which reminds us that we do
not live on bread alone.

Silence.

Out of the silence the cantor sings, quietly:

> Praise him for our harvest store
> He hath filled the garner floor
> For his mercies aye endure
> Ever faithful, ever sure.

*The members repeat the verse, singing quietly. The musical
instrument continues as a member of the community walks
to the table with a carton or bottle of milk. The leader says,
over the music:*

The gift of milk.

You open your hand

All   **And fill all things living with plenteousness.**

Member   I present to God this milk, on behalf of all
of us, as a token of our gratitude for his
loving care of us and as a symbol of human
warmth and kindness to be shown to
children, to those in our community who
are wounded on the human journey, and all
who are disadvantaged in *our* society and
other societies.

Silence.

Out of the silence, the cantor sings:

> All things living he doth feed
> His full hand supplies their need
> For his mercies aye endure
> Ever faithful, ever sure.

The members repeat the verse, singing quietly. The musical instrument continues as a young member walks to the table with a piece of fruit and a vegetable. The leader says, over the music:

> The gift of fruit and vegetables.
>
> He brought forth grass for the cattle

All   **And green herbs for the service of men.**

Member   I offer to God, on behalf of all of us, fruits of the earth as a token of the new life of the future entrusted to us. Let us pray for our schools, our youth organizations, especially *N* (and *N*), that we may grow to realize our future potential and come a little nearer to the stature of Christ.

Silence.

Out of the silence the cantor sings:

> And hath bid the fruitful field
> Crops of precious increase yield
> For his mercies aye endure
> Ever faithful, ever sure.

The members repeat the verse, singing quietly. The musical instrument continues as a member of the community walks to the table with an artefact representing manufacturing industry. The leader says, over the music:

The gift of industry.

Whatever your hand finds to do

All **Do with all your might.**

Member   I offer to God, on behalf of all of us, this industrial product, as a token of the gifts of craft and skill that he has given us. Let us pray that there may be in industry and commerce a freedom from distrust, an absolute integrity, and a search for what is just.

Silence.

Out of the silence, the cantor sings:

God with all-commanding might
Filled the new-made world with light.
For his mercies aye endure
Ever faithful, ever sure.

The musical instrument continues as the treasurer walks to the table with money. The leader says, over the music:

The gift of money.

Bear one another's burdens

All **And so fulfil the law of Christ.**

| Treasurer | I present the offering of this Christian community as a token of our possessions which are all a trust from God. Lord, we ask that this community may be known for its industry, its stillness, its right use of leisure, its sacrificial giving and its honest dealing. May we come to love you more and more — and the people you give to us to care for. |

Silence.

Out of the silence, the cantor sings in a firm voice:

> Let us blaze his name abroad
> For of gods he is the God
> For his mercies aye endure
> Ever faithful, ever sure.

The members sing more loudly:

> And for richer food than this
> Pledge of everlasting bliss
> For his mercies aye endure
> Ever faithful, ever sure.

The members complete the time of prayer by singing at full volume:

> Glory to our bounteous King
> Glory let creation sing
> For his mercies aye endure
> Ever faithful, ever sure.

A profound silence is kept by the community.

THE BIDDINGS AND THE COLLECTS

I would guess that this is the most usual way of conducting intercessions in public worship — a bidding which is written down or just spoken 'off the cuff', followed by a formal prayer which complements and amplifies the subject matter of the bidding. I have written about the care which needs to be taken over biddings. Equal care is needed in the selection of collects, in terms of style, language, and progression of thinking. The compilations of Canon Frank Colquhoun, *Parish Prayers* and *Contemporary Parish Prayers* in particular, are still hard to beat. Michael Hollings, Etta Gullick and Bishop George Appleton are more than runners-up because their work is more original, creative, fresh than Canon Colquhoun's essential tidiness! The magisterial *Oxford Book of Prayer*, edited by George Appleton, is severely disabled by a very poor subject index, which makes it difficult to use.

INTERCESSIONS WITH MUSIC

Prayers interspersed with music, or prayers which are virtually all music, with cantor and response, have been popularized by the religious communities, notably Taizé and Iona.

For those of you not familiar with this strain of worship, here is a Taizé intercession which may be used with any of the Taizé settings of *Kyrie eleison* (Lord have mercy). These can be found in *Songs and Prayers from Taizé* (Mowbray), nos 4, 5 or 6.

Intercession: prayers for all humanity

Kyrie eleison
- O Christ, your life was not spectacular: you
  carried a cross: help us walk along your road . . .
  Kyrie eleison
- O Christ, you learned faithfulness by suffering:
  you have become a source of eternal salvation . . .
  Kyrie eleison
- O Christ, when wounded you did not make
  threats: show us how to forgive to the very end . . .
  Kyrie eleison
- O Christ, when forced to suffer you did not rebel:
  transfigure our refusals . . .
  Kyrie eleison
- O Christ, you see our suffering and failures: help
  us walk along your road . . .
  Kyrie eleison
- O Christ, you see the pain of the exiled and the
  abandoned: take their suffering upon yourself . . .
  Kyrie eleison
- O Christ, when lies and worries tempt us
  to forsake you, your Holy Spirit remains always
  within us . . .
  Kyrie eleison
- O Christ, when our hearts become heavy, make
  them transparent like a springtime in flower . . .
  Kyrie eleison
- O Christ, you bring happiness to your servants:
  enable us to live rooted in your trust . . .
  Kyrie eleison
- O Christ, our life is hidden with you in God; your
  joy penetrates to the depths of our souls . . .
  Kyrie eleison

  Taizé

Other material may be used in the same way: each suffrage can be chanted to good effect and then followed by the singing of the simple response or refrain, set to an immediately accessible tune and sung by the whole congregation.

Many other intercessions in this style can be found in another book from Mowbray, *Songs and Prayers of the Church*, compiled by John Michael Mountney, who contributes many of them himself.

EXTEMPORE

This usually means that a priest, a minister, a worship leader conducts all the prayers using his or her own words extempore. Often there are no silences and no one else speaks or sings. Obviously the dangers lie in 'waffle', 'blathering', repetition and such like. But to hear it done well is to hear the operation of a great gift. Some Free Church ministers have the gift (and the training), and it brings a penetrating devotion. I always doubt that it is truly extempore, truly of the moment, truly the Holy Spirit 'who shall give you what to say'. I sense that the most inspiring efforts have been prayed and learned elsewhere, and are then not parroted by heart but *really* prayed in the public domain. Beware!

CONCLUSION

As I have said, prayer is intensely personal. So you will choose a way which suits you. It is boring to say this, but, whatever method you use, use it with real care, for the privilege of leading other people's prayers is great. Sometimes we exercise great care over the preparation of material which will give the honour to ourselves (sermons, for example), where we perform solo, and not enough to the galvanic community contribution. We sense that this is wrong.

ACKNOWLEDGEMENTS

The author wishes to express his thanks to the following for permission to use or adapt material of which they are authors, publishers or copyright holders.

Intercessions from the Alternative Service Book 1980 © Central Board of Finance of the Church of England. Reproduced with permission.

The Most Revd George Appleton

B. T. Batsford for the prayer from *Prayers for Today*, ed. John Elphinstone-Fyffe (© B. T. Batsford Ltd 1958).

BBC Books for prayers taken and adapted from *New Every Morning*

The Cambridge Pastorate

The Church Missionary Society for the prayer from *With All Our Strength*

Canon Frank Colquhoun

The Right Revd Timothy Dudley-Smith

Harper and Row for 'Litany for All Workers' by Reinhold Niebuhr, published in *The Wideness of God's Mercy*, ed. Jeffrey W. Rowthorn (The Seabury Press)

James Jordan

The Mothers' Union for the prayer by Joan Kendall

Mowbray for the prayer from F. D. MacNutt, *The Prayer Manual*

Basil Naylor

St Andrew Press for the prayer adapted from *Worship Now*

St Martin-in-the-Fields, London

SLG Press for the prayer by Sister Ruth SLG

The Taizé Community for the intercession from *Songs and Prayers from Taizé*

The Right Revd Maurice Wood

If the compiler has unwittingly transgressed any copyright, he makes sincere apologies and will acknowledge any such oversights in future editions.